Easy Delightful Valentine's Day

Supper Recipes

Marshella Goodsworth

Copy right 2013 by Marshella Goodsworth

Dedication

Dedicated to the Lord who has given

me a love for cooking and for helping

orphan children

Easy Delightful Valentine's Day

Supper Recipes

Marshella Goodsworth

Make quick, easy, delicious meals for your special Valentine's Day.

Recipes you will find here:

Delicious Broccoli Pasta Casserole a La Deluxe de Feta

Fabulous Fettuccine Accented With the Decadence of Wild Mushrooms

Luscious Lamb With Mango and Mint Salsa

Sassy Salmon a La Vinaigrette de Rosemary and Sage

Classic Timeless Roasted Chicken with a Hint of Summer Savoury, Served with Carrots, Green Beans and Young

Potatoes

♥♥♥

*Delicious Broccoli Pasta Casserole a
La Deluxe de Feta*

1 1/2 tablespoons of olive oil

1/2 tablespoon of canola oil

2 red onions finely chopped

1 red bell pepper diced

3/4 teaspoon of black pepper

2 cans of Italian tomatoes (can size--28 ounces)

2 cups of apple juice

1 1/2 teaspoons of salt

4 bunches of broccoli

32 ounces of rotini pasta

1 cup of crumbled feta cheese

1 cup of grated cheddar cheese

1/3 cup of grated mozzarella cheese (optional)

12 slices of cooked crisp bacon

crumbled

1/4 cup of raisins

1/4 cup of sesame seeds

3/4 cup of Italian dressing

2 teaspoons of dried oregano

3 tablespoons of margarine

In a large frying pan, over medium heat, warm oil, add onions and red pepper.

Add tomatoes and apple juice.

Bring to a boil, breaking up tomatoes with a spoon.

Reduce heat to medium-low.

Simmer sauce for 13 minutes,

until it thickens.

Stir in salt and pepper.

Meanwhile in a large pot, bring salted water to a boil.

Add broccoli.

Cook broccoli for seven minutes, until tender-crisp.

Using a slotted spoon, transfer broccoli to a bowl.

Toss broccoli with margarine.

Add pasta to water and cook until al dente, about 9 minutes.

Drain pasta.

Heat broccoli for 1 minute in microwave to heat through.

Mix broccoli and all other ingredients with pasta.

Serve and enjoy.

Fabulous Fettuccine Accented With the Decadence of Wild Mushrooms

1 1/2 tablespoons of canola oil

6 spicy bologna or 12 slices of bacon

diced

1 leek

1 red bell pepper

2 green onions

1 teaspoon of dried thyme

1/3 teaspoon of salt

1/4 teaspoon of black pepper

1 1/4 cup of chicken broth

12 ounces of dried fettuccine

1/2 cup of grated mozzarella cheese

7 cups of wild mushrooms, such as chanterelles, shiitake, and/or cremini sliced

1 cup of dried cranberries

1 can of cream of broccoli soup

1/3 cup of mayonnaise

In a large frying pan, over medium heat, warm oil.

Add bologna or bacon and sauté

for 2 minutes or longer for bacon if needed.

Add bell pepper and leek.

Sauté for 3 minutes.

Add mushrooms, sat and pepper.

Cook until tender, for about 6 minutes.

Increase heat to medium-high.

Add broth and green onions.

Simmer until syrupy, about 4 minutes.

Meanwhile cook pasta according to package directions.

Drain pasta.

Add to mushroom mixture.

Stir in remaining ingredients.

Serve and enjoy.

Luscious Lamb With Mango and Mint Salsa (Note: Pork chops may be used in place of lamb chops)

1/4 cup of fresh mint leaves

1/4 cup of baby spinach leaves

2 green onions coarsely chopped

1/4 teaspoon of salt

2 mangoes, peeled and cut into chunks

Dash of pepper

1 teaspoon of sugar

1 teaspoon of grated orange zest

2 Tablespoons of orange juice

Dash of dried oregano

1/3 teaspoon of black pepper

Drizzle of balsamic vinegar

1/2 cup of extra-virgin olive oil

*4 lamb chops or pork chops (shoulder,
round bone for lamb chops)*

*For salsa, mix all ingredients in
food processor.*

*Sprinkle lamb with salt and
pepper.*

Place in shallow baking dish

with about 1 to 2 inches of water.

Bake in oven for 30 to 35 minutes.

Top with salsa.

Serve and enjoy.

Sassy Salmon a La Vinaigrette de

Rosemary and Sage

2 teaspoons of sweet mustard

2 teaspoons of white grape juice

*1 tablespoon of club soda or lemon-
lime soda*

*3 tablespoons of canola oil, plus more
as needed*

1 red onion minced

1/2 teaspoon dried rosemary

1/2 teaspoon of dried sage

2 teaspoons of pineapple juice

1/3 teaspoon of black pepper

2 salmon fillets

4 cups of diced potatoes, cooked and cooled

1/2 cup of Russian dressing

3 cups of mixed salad greens

Mix first nine ingredients together for vinaigrette to serve on top of salmon.

Brush baking dish for salmon with oil.

Place skin side of salmon down in baking dish.

Spoon the vinaigrette over salmon.

Marinate at room temperature for 35 minutes.

Preheat oven to 400 degrees Fahrenheit and cook salmon for 20 to 30 minutes.

In a bowl, toss salad greens, potatoes and Russian dressing. Season with salt and pepper as desired.

Brush melted butter or margarine over salmon once it is done.

Serve meal and enjoy.

♥♥♥

Classic Timeless Roasted Chicken with a Hint of Summer Savoury, Served with Carrots, Green Beans and Young Potatoes

4 pound chicken

2 red onions sliced in rounds

2 teaspoons of summer savoury

1 1/2 teaspoons of salt

1/2 teaspoon of pepper

1 1/2 pounds of new potatoes halved

5 carrots cut into 3 inch pieces

1/2 pound of fresh green beans

2 1/4 tablespoons of canola oil

3/4 cup of white grape juice

Preheat oven to 425 degrees F.

Grease heavy large rimmed baking dish.

Wash chicken and pat dry with paper towels.

Starting at edge of cavity, slide finger under skin over each breast half, making pockets.

Place half teaspoon of summer savoury in each pocket.

Sprinkle remaining summer savoury over chicken.

Season with half the salt and pepper.

Place onions over chicken.

Roast chicken for about 30 to 40 minutes.

Meanwhile in a bowl, toss potatoes, carrots and beans with oil, and remaining salt and pepper.

After chicken has roasted for 30 to 40 minutes, remove from oven.

Tilt pan and spoon off most of fat.

Arrange chicken in center of pan.

Spoon vegetables around the chicken, turning potatoes, cut side down.

Return pan to oven.

Roast until chicken juices run clear when meat is pierced, about 40 to 50 minutes, longer.

Transfer chicken and vegetables to platter to rest.

Pour pan juices into pot.

Skim fat.

Add grape juice to pan.

Set pan over medium heat.

Bring to a boil.

Stir up any browned bits.

Pour into pot.

Boil until reduced slightly--
about 4 to 6 minutes.

Add any juices from chicken platter.

Mix in 1/4 teaspoon of dried oregano and 1/2 teaspoon of dried basil.

Thicken with a bit of potato starch if desired.

Serve with chicken and

vegetables.

Serve and enjoy.